50 Middle Eastern Salad Recipes for Home

By: Kelly Johnson

Table of Contents

- Tabouleh
- Fattoush
- Tabbouleh
- Fattoush
- Shirazi Salad
- Greek Salad
- Arabic Salad
- Persian Salad
- Israeli Salad
- Turkish Shepherd's Salad
- Cucumber Tomato Salad
- Lebanese Fattoush
- Moroccan Carrot Salad
- Eggplant Salad (Baba Ganoush)
- Beetroot Salad
- Chickpea Salad
- Lentil Salad
- Potato Salad with Middle Eastern Twist
- Tuna Salad with Mediterranean Flavors
- Spinach Salad with Pomegranate Dressing
- Radish Salad with Sumac Dressing
- Watermelon Salad with Feta Cheese
- Orange and Olive Salad
- Cauliflower Salad with Tahini Dressing
- Grilled Halloumi Salad
- Avocado and Chickpea Salad
- Quinoa Tabbouleh
- Labneh Salad with Mint and Olives
- Artichoke Salad
- Green Bean Salad with Almonds
- Kale Salad with Za'atar Dressing
- Date and Walnut Salad
- Bulgur Salad with Herbs
- Roasted Pepper Salad
- Cabbage Salad with Lemon-Tahini Dressing

- Arugula Salad with Figs and Goat Cheese
- Zucchini Salad with Yogurt Dressing
- Pistachio and Cranberry Couscous Salad
- Tzatziki Cucumber Salad
- Carrot and Raisin Salad
- Chickpea and Spinach Salad
- Watercress Salad with Citrus Dressing
- Millet Salad with Roasted Vegetables
- Egg Salad with Middle Eastern Spices
- Radicchio and Orange Salad
- Black Bean Salad with Cilantro-Lime Dressing
- Mushroom Salad with Balsamic Glaze
- Roasted Tomato Salad
- Asparagus Salad with Lemon-Parmesan Dressing
- Lentil and Roasted Vegetable Salad

Tabouleh

Ingredients:

- 1 cup bulgur wheat
- 1 1/2 cups boiling water
- 3 cups fresh parsley, finely chopped
- 1 cup fresh mint leaves, finely chopped
- 2 medium tomatoes, diced
- 1/2 cup green onions, thinly sliced
- 1/4 cup lemon juice
- 1/4 cup extra virgin olive oil
- Salt and pepper to taste

Instructions:

Place the bulgur wheat in a large bowl and pour the boiling water over it. Cover the bowl with a lid or plastic wrap and let it sit for about 30 minutes, or until the bulgur is tender and has absorbed all the water.
Fluff the bulgur with a fork and let it cool to room temperature.
Once the bulgur is cooled, add the chopped parsley, mint, tomatoes, and green onions to the bowl.
In a separate small bowl, whisk together the lemon juice, olive oil, salt, and pepper.
Pour the dressing over the salad and toss everything together until well combined and evenly coated.
Taste and adjust seasoning if needed.
Cover the tabouleh and refrigerate for at least 1 hour before serving to allow the flavors to meld together.
Serve chilled or at room temperature as a side dish or a light meal.

Enjoy your fresh and flavorful tabouleh salad!

Fattoush

Ingredients:

For the Salad:

- 2 medium cucumbers, diced
- 4 medium tomatoes, diced
- 1 green bell pepper, diced
- 1 red onion, thinly sliced
- 1 cup radishes, thinly sliced
- 1 cup fresh parsley, chopped
- 1 cup fresh mint leaves, chopped
- 2 cups romaine lettuce, torn into bite-sized pieces
- 2 pieces of pita bread, toasted or fried until crispy, then broken into small pieces
- Optional: 1 cup chopped fresh vegetables such as green onions, celery, or carrots

For the Dressing:

- 1/4 cup extra virgin olive oil
- 3 tablespoons lemon juice
- 1 garlic clove, minced
- 1 teaspoon sumac (optional)
- Salt and pepper to taste

Instructions:

In a large salad bowl, combine the diced cucumbers, tomatoes, bell pepper, red onion, radishes, parsley, mint, romaine lettuce, and any additional chopped vegetables you're using.
Add the crispy pieces of pita bread to the bowl.
In a small bowl, whisk together the olive oil, lemon juice, minced garlic, sumac (if using), salt, and pepper to make the dressing.
Pour the dressing over the salad and toss everything together until well coated.
Taste and adjust seasoning if needed.
Let the salad sit for about 10-15 minutes before serving to allow the flavors to meld together.

Serve the fattoush salad as a refreshing side dish or light meal.

Enjoy your delicious homemade fattoush salad!

Tabbouleh

Ingredients:

- 1/2 cup bulgur wheat
- 1 cup boiling water
- 3 cups fresh flat-leaf parsley, finely chopped
- 1/2 cup fresh mint leaves, finely chopped
- 2 medium tomatoes, diced
- 1/2 cup green onions or scallions, thinly sliced
- 1/4 cup red onion, finely chopped
- 1/4 cup extra virgin olive oil
- 1/4 cup fresh lemon juice
- Salt and freshly ground black pepper, to taste

Optional:

- 1/2 cup cucumber, diced
- 1/2 cup bell pepper, diced

Instructions:

Place the bulgur wheat in a heatproof bowl and pour the boiling water over it. Cover the bowl with a lid or plastic wrap and let it sit for about 20-30 minutes, or until the bulgur is tender and has absorbed all the water. Drain any excess water if necessary.
In a large mixing bowl, combine the chopped parsley, mint, tomatoes, green onions, and red onion. If using cucumber and bell pepper, add them as well.
Once the bulgur is ready, add it to the bowl with the vegetables.
In a small bowl, whisk together the olive oil, lemon juice, salt, and pepper to make the dressing.
Pour the dressing over the tabbouleh mixture and toss everything together until well combined and evenly coated.
Taste and adjust seasoning if needed.
Cover the tabbouleh and refrigerate for at least 1 hour before serving to allow the flavors to meld together.
Serve chilled or at room temperature as a side dish or a light meal.

Enjoy your fresh and flavorful tabbouleh salad!

Fattoush

Ingredients:

For the Salad:

- 2 large tomatoes, diced
- 1 cucumber, diced
- 1 green bell pepper, diced
- 1 red onion, thinly sliced
- 1 cup radishes, thinly sliced
- 1 cup fresh parsley leaves, chopped
- 1 cup fresh mint leaves, chopped
- 2 pieces of pita bread, toasted or fried until crispy
- Optional: 1 cup chopped romaine lettuce or other salad greens

For the Dressing:

- 1/4 cup extra virgin olive oil
- 3 tablespoons fresh lemon juice
- 1 garlic clove, minced
- 1 teaspoon sumac (optional)
- Salt and freshly ground black pepper, to taste

Instructions:

In a large salad bowl, combine the diced tomatoes, cucumber, bell pepper, red onion, radishes, parsley, mint, and optional salad greens.
Break the crispy pita bread into bite-sized pieces and add them to the bowl.
In a small bowl, whisk together the olive oil, lemon juice, minced garlic, sumac (if using), salt, and pepper to make the dressing.
Pour the dressing over the salad and toss everything together until well coated.
Taste and adjust seasoning if needed.
Let the salad sit for about 10-15 minutes before serving to allow the flavors to meld together.
Serve the fattoush salad as a refreshing side dish or light meal.

Enjoy your delicious homemade fattoush salad!

Shirazi Salad

Ingredients:

- 2 large cucumbers, diced
- 2 large tomatoes, diced
- 1 small red onion, finely chopped
- 1/4 cup fresh mint leaves, chopped
- 1/4 cup fresh parsley leaves, chopped
- Juice of 1-2 lemons, to taste
- 2 tablespoons extra virgin olive oil
- Salt and freshly ground black pepper, to taste

Instructions:

In a large salad bowl, combine the diced cucumbers, tomatoes, red onion, chopped mint, and chopped parsley.
Drizzle the lemon juice and olive oil over the salad.
Season with salt and freshly ground black pepper, to taste.
Toss everything together until well combined and evenly coated with the dressing.
Taste and adjust seasoning if needed, adding more lemon juice, olive oil, salt, or pepper as desired.
Let the Shirazi salad sit for about 10-15 minutes before serving to allow the flavors to meld together.
Serve the salad as a refreshing side dish or as part of a mezze spread alongside other Middle Eastern dishes.

Enjoy your delicious and vibrant Shirazi salad!

Greek Salad

Ingredients:

- 2 large tomatoes, cut into wedges
- 1 cucumber, sliced
- 1 red onion, thinly sliced
- 1 green bell pepper, sliced
- 1/2 cup Kalamata olives, pitted
- 4 ounces feta cheese, crumbled
- 1/4 cup extra virgin olive oil
- 2 tablespoons red wine vinegar or fresh lemon juice
- 1 teaspoon dried oregano
- Salt and freshly ground black pepper, to taste

Instructions:

In a large salad bowl, combine the tomato wedges, sliced cucumber, thinly sliced red onion, sliced green bell pepper, and Kalamata olives.
In a small bowl, whisk together the extra virgin olive oil, red wine vinegar or lemon juice, dried oregano, salt, and freshly ground black pepper to make the dressing.
Pour the dressing over the salad ingredients in the bowl.
Toss everything together gently until well combined and evenly coated with the dressing.
Crumble the feta cheese over the top of the salad.
Taste and adjust seasoning if needed, adding more salt, pepper, or vinegar according to your preference.
Let the Greek salad sit for about 10-15 minutes before serving to allow the flavors to meld together.
Serve the salad as a refreshing side dish or as part of a Mediterranean-inspired meal.

Enjoy your delicious homemade Greek salad!

Arabic Salad

Ingredients:

- 2 large tomatoes, diced
- 1 cucumber, diced
- 1 red onion, thinly sliced
- 1 green bell pepper, diced
- 1/2 cup fresh parsley leaves, chopped
- 1/4 cup fresh mint leaves, chopped (optional)
- Juice of 1-2 lemons, to taste
- 2 tablespoons extra virgin olive oil
- Salt and freshly ground black pepper, to taste

Instructions:

In a large salad bowl, combine the diced tomatoes, cucumber, sliced red onion, diced green bell pepper, chopped parsley, and optional chopped mint leaves.
Drizzle the lemon juice and extra virgin olive oil over the salad.
Season with salt and freshly ground black pepper, to taste.
Toss everything together until well combined and evenly coated with the dressing.
Taste and adjust seasoning if needed, adding more lemon juice, olive oil, salt, or pepper as desired.
Let the Arabic salad sit for about 10-15 minutes before serving to allow the flavors to meld together.
Serve the salad as a refreshing side dish or as part of a Middle Eastern meal.

Enjoy your delicious and colorful Arabic salad!

Persian Salad

Ingredients:

- 2 large cucumbers, diced
- 2 large tomatoes, diced
- 1/2 red onion, finely chopped
- 1/4 cup fresh mint leaves, chopped
- 1/4 cup fresh parsley leaves, chopped
- Juice of 1-2 lemons, to taste
- 2 tablespoons extra virgin olive oil
- Salt and freshly ground black pepper, to taste

Instructions:

In a large salad bowl, combine the diced cucumbers, tomatoes, chopped red onion, chopped mint, and chopped parsley.
Drizzle the lemon juice and extra virgin olive oil over the salad.
Season with salt and freshly ground black pepper, to taste.
Toss everything together until well combined and evenly coated with the dressing.
Taste and adjust seasoning if needed, adding more lemon juice, olive oil, salt, or pepper as desired.
Let the Persian salad sit for about 10-15 minutes before serving to allow the flavors to meld together.
Serve the salad as a refreshing side dish or as part of a Persian-inspired meal.

Enjoy your delicious and vibrant Persian salad!

Israeli Salad

Ingredients:

- 2 large tomatoes, diced
- 1 cucumber, diced
- 1 bell pepper (any color), diced
- 1/2 red onion, finely chopped
- 1/4 cup fresh parsley leaves, chopped
- Juice of 1-2 lemons, to taste
- 2 tablespoons extra virgin olive oil
- Salt and freshly ground black pepper, to taste

Instructions:

In a large salad bowl, combine the diced tomatoes, cucumber, bell pepper, chopped red onion, and chopped parsley.
Drizzle the lemon juice and extra virgin olive oil over the salad.
Season with salt and freshly ground black pepper, to taste.
Toss everything together until well combined and evenly coated with the dressing.
Taste and adjust seasoning if needed, adding more lemon juice, olive oil, salt, or pepper as desired.
Let the Israeli salad sit for about 10-15 minutes before serving to allow the flavors to meld together.
Serve the salad as a refreshing side dish or as part of a Mediterranean-inspired meal.

Enjoy your delicious and colorful Israeli salad!

Turkish Shepherd's Salad

Ingredients:

- 2 large tomatoes, diced
- 1 cucumber, diced
- 1 green bell pepper, diced
- 1 red onion, finely chopped
- 1/4 cup chopped fresh parsley
- 1/4 cup extra virgin olive oil
- 2 tablespoons freshly squeezed lemon juice
- Salt and freshly ground black pepper to taste
- Optional: olives, feta cheese

Instructions:

In a large mixing bowl, combine the diced tomatoes, cucumber, bell pepper, chopped onion, and parsley.
Drizzle the olive oil and lemon juice over the salad.
Season with salt and black pepper according to your taste preferences.
Gently toss all the ingredients together until well combined.
Taste and adjust seasoning if necessary.
If desired, garnish the salad with olives and crumbled feta cheese before serving.
Serve the Turkish Shepherd's Salad chilled or at room temperature as a refreshing side dish or as part of a mezze spread.

This salad is best enjoyed fresh and can be served alongside grilled meats, kebabs, or as a light appetizer before a main course. It's a versatile dish that can be customized to suit your taste by adding other vegetables or ingredients like mint, oregano, or even a dash of sumac for extra flavor. Enjoy!

Cucumber Tomato Salad

Ingredients:

- 2 large tomatoes, diced
- 1 English cucumber or 2-3 Persian cucumbers, diced
- 1/4 cup red onion, thinly sliced (optional)
- 2 tablespoons fresh parsley or basil, chopped
- 2 tablespoons extra virgin olive oil
- 1 tablespoon red wine vinegar or freshly squeezed lemon juice
- Salt and freshly ground black pepper to taste
- Optional: crumbled feta cheese, olives, diced avocado

Instructions:

In a large mixing bowl, combine the diced tomatoes, diced cucumber, sliced red onion (if using), and chopped parsley or basil.
Drizzle the extra virgin olive oil and red wine vinegar or lemon juice over the salad.
Season with salt and black pepper according to your taste preferences.
Gently toss all the ingredients together until well combined.
Taste and adjust seasoning if necessary.
If desired, garnish the salad with crumbled feta cheese, olives, or diced avocado before serving.
Serve the cucumber tomato salad chilled or at room temperature as a refreshing side dish or as part of a picnic or barbecue spread.

This salad is versatile and can be customized to suit your taste. You can add other ingredients like bell peppers, red pepper flakes for heat, or even a sprinkle of dried herbs like oregano or thyme for extra flavor. Enjoy this light and delicious salad!

Lebanese Fattoush

Ingredients:

For the Salad:

- 2 large tomatoes, diced
- 1 cucumber, diced
- 1 red bell pepper, diced
- 1 green bell pepper, diced
- 1 small red onion, thinly sliced
- 1 cup chopped romaine lettuce or other salad greens
- 1/4 cup chopped fresh mint leaves
- 1/4 cup chopped fresh parsley
- 1 cup toasted pita bread, torn into bite-sized pieces

For the Dressing:

- 1/4 cup extra virgin olive oil
- 2 tablespoons freshly squeezed lemon juice
- 1 tablespoon pomegranate molasses (optional)
- 1 garlic clove, minced
- 1 teaspoon sumac (optional)
- Salt and freshly ground black pepper to taste

Instructions:

In a large mixing bowl, combine the diced tomatoes, diced cucumber, diced bell peppers, thinly sliced red onion, chopped lettuce, chopped mint, chopped parsley, and torn pita bread pieces.
In a separate small bowl, whisk together the extra virgin olive oil, freshly squeezed lemon juice, pomegranate molasses (if using), minced garlic, sumac (if using), salt, and black pepper to make the dressing.
Pour the dressing over the salad ingredients in the large mixing bowl.
Gently toss all the ingredients together until well coated with the dressing.
Taste and adjust seasoning if necessary.
Let the salad sit for a few minutes to allow the flavors to meld together.

Serve the Lebanese Fattoush salad immediately, garnished with additional fresh herbs or a sprinkle of sumac if desired.

Fattoush is best served fresh and can be enjoyed as a light and nutritious meal on its own or as a side dish alongside grilled meats or other Middle Eastern dishes. It's a versatile salad that can also be customized with additional ingredients such as radishes, green onions, or even grilled halloumi cheese. Enjoy!

Moroccan Carrot Salad

Ingredients:

- 4 large carrots, peeled and grated
- 1/4 cup raisins or chopped dates
- 1/4 cup chopped fresh cilantro or parsley
- 1/4 cup chopped almonds or walnuts (optional, for extra crunch)
- 2 tablespoons olive oil
- 2 tablespoons freshly squeezed lemon juice
- 1 teaspoon honey or maple syrup
- 1/2 teaspoon ground cumin
- 1/2 teaspoon ground cinnamon
- 1/4 teaspoon ground ginger
- Salt and freshly ground black pepper to taste
- Optional: pinch of cayenne pepper for heat

Instructions:

In a large mixing bowl, combine the grated carrots, raisins or chopped dates, chopped cilantro or parsley, and chopped almonds or walnuts (if using).
In a small bowl, whisk together the olive oil, lemon juice, honey or maple syrup, ground cumin, ground cinnamon, ground ginger, salt, black pepper, and cayenne pepper (if using).
Pour the dressing over the carrot mixture in the large mixing bowl.
Gently toss all the ingredients together until well coated with the dressing.
Taste and adjust seasoning if necessary.
Let the salad sit for at least 15-20 minutes before serving to allow the flavors to meld together.
Serve the Moroccan Carrot Salad chilled or at room temperature as a flavorful side dish or appetizer.

This salad can be made ahead of time and stored in the refrigerator for a few hours before serving. The flavors will continue to develop over time, making it even more delicious. Enjoy the combination of sweet, savory, and spicy flavors in this Moroccan-inspired salad!

Eggplant Salad (Baba Ganoush)

Ingredients:

- 2 medium-sized eggplants
- 2 cloves of garlic, minced
- 2 tablespoons tahini
- 2 tablespoons lemon juice
- 2 tablespoons olive oil
- Salt, to taste
- Optional: chopped fresh parsley, paprika, or olive oil for garnish

Instructions:

Preheat your oven to 400°F (200°C).
Wash the eggplants and pierce them with a fork in several places.
Place the eggplants on a baking sheet lined with parchment paper and bake for about 40-45 minutes, or until the eggplants are completely soft and collapsed.
Once the eggplants are done, remove them from the oven and let them cool for a few minutes until they are cool enough to handle.
Peel off the skin from the eggplants and discard it. Place the flesh of the eggplants in a colander to drain excess liquid for about 10-15 minutes.
In a mixing bowl, mash the drained eggplant flesh using a fork or a potato masher until smooth.
Add minced garlic, tahini, lemon juice, olive oil, and salt to the mashed eggplant, and mix well until all the ingredients are fully incorporated.
Taste and adjust seasoning if needed.
Transfer the eggplant salad to a serving bowl, drizzle with a little more olive oil, and garnish with chopped fresh parsley or a sprinkle of paprika if desired.
Serve the Baba Ganoush with pita bread, crackers, or vegetable sticks for dipping.

Enjoy your homemade Eggplant Salad!

Beetroot Salad

Ingredients:

- 3 medium-sized beetroots, cooked and peeled
- 2 tablespoons olive oil
- 1 tablespoon balsamic vinegar
- 1 tablespoon honey
- 2 cloves garlic, minced
- Salt and pepper, to taste
- 2 tablespoons chopped fresh parsley (optional)
- 1/4 cup crumbled feta cheese (optional)

Instructions:

Begin by cooking the beetroots. You can either roast them in the oven or boil them until they are tender. Once cooked, let them cool completely before handling.

Once the beetroots are cooled, peel off the skin and chop them into bite-sized cubes or slices, depending on your preference. Place them in a mixing bowl.

In a small bowl, whisk together olive oil, balsamic vinegar, honey, minced garlic, salt, and pepper until well combined.

Pour the dressing over the chopped beetroots in the mixing bowl and toss gently until the beetroots are evenly coated.

If using, sprinkle chopped fresh parsley and crumbled feta cheese over the salad and toss lightly.

Taste the salad and adjust the seasoning if needed.

Transfer the beetroot salad to a serving dish and serve immediately, or refrigerate for a couple of hours to allow the flavors to meld together before serving.

Enjoy your refreshing Beetroot Salad as a side dish or a light lunch option!

Feel free to adjust the ingredients according to your taste preferences, adding more or less honey, vinegar, or garlic as desired.

Chickpea Salad

Ingredients:

- 2 cans (15 ounces each) chickpeas (garbanzo beans), drained and rinsed
- 1 cucumber, diced
- 1 bell pepper (any color), diced
- 1/2 red onion, finely chopped
- 1 cup cherry tomatoes, halved
- 1/4 cup chopped fresh parsley
- 1/4 cup chopped fresh cilantro (optional)
- Juice of 1 lemon
- 2 tablespoons extra-virgin olive oil
- 1 teaspoon ground cumin
- Salt and black pepper, to taste
- Optional add-ins: diced avocado, crumbled feta cheese, chopped olives, chopped jalapeños

Instructions:

In a large mixing bowl, combine the drained and rinsed chickpeas, diced cucumber, diced bell pepper, chopped red onion, halved cherry tomatoes, chopped parsley, and cilantro (if using).
In a small bowl, whisk together the lemon juice, extra-virgin olive oil, ground cumin, salt, and black pepper until well combined.
Pour the dressing over the chickpea mixture in the large bowl and toss gently to coat all the ingredients evenly.
Taste the salad and adjust the seasoning if needed.
If desired, add any optional add-ins such as diced avocado, crumbled feta cheese, chopped olives, or chopped jalapeños and toss gently to combine.
Transfer the Chickpea Salad to a serving dish and serve immediately, or refrigerate for about 30 minutes to allow the flavors to meld together before serving.
Enjoy your delicious and protein-packed Chickpea Salad as a side dish, light lunch, or even as a filling for wraps or pitas!

This salad is versatile, so feel free to customize it with your favorite vegetables and add-ins. You can also adjust the quantities of the ingredients according to your taste preferences.

Lentil Salad

Ingredients:

- 1 cup dried green or brown lentils
- 2 cups water or vegetable broth
- 1 cucumber, diced
- 1 bell pepper (any color), diced
- 1/2 red onion, finely chopped
- 1 cup cherry tomatoes, halved
- 1/4 cup chopped fresh parsley
- Juice of 1 lemon
- 3 tablespoons extra-virgin olive oil
- 2 cloves garlic, minced
- 1 teaspoon Dijon mustard
- Salt and black pepper, to taste
- Optional: crumbled feta cheese, chopped olives, chopped fresh basil, chopped fresh mint

Instructions:

Rinse the lentils under cold water in a fine-mesh sieve.
In a medium saucepan, combine the rinsed lentils and water or vegetable broth. Bring to a boil over high heat, then reduce the heat to low, cover, and simmer for about 20-25 minutes, or until the lentils are tender but still hold their shape. Drain any excess liquid and let the lentils cool slightly.
In a large mixing bowl, combine the cooked lentils, diced cucumber, diced bell pepper, chopped red onion, halved cherry tomatoes, and chopped parsley.
In a small bowl, whisk together the lemon juice, extra-virgin olive oil, minced garlic, Dijon mustard, salt, and black pepper until well combined.
Pour the dressing over the lentil mixture in the large bowl and toss gently to coat all the ingredients evenly.
Taste the salad and adjust the seasoning if needed.

If desired, add optional ingredients such as crumbled feta cheese, chopped olives, chopped fresh basil, or chopped fresh mint and toss gently to combine. Transfer the Lentil Salad to a serving dish and serve immediately, or refrigerate for about 30 minutes to allow the flavors to meld together before serving.
Enjoy your nutritious and satisfying Lentil Salad as a side dish, light lunch, or even as a filling for wraps or sandwiches!

Feel free to customize this salad with your favorite vegetables and add-ins, or adjust the quantities of the ingredients according to your taste preferences.

Potato Salad with Middle Eastern Twist

Ingredients:

- 2 lbs (about 900g) potatoes, preferably Yukon Gold or similar variety, peeled and cut into bite-sized cubes
- 1/2 cup plain Greek yogurt
- 2 tablespoons tahini
- 2 tablespoons lemon juice
- 2 cloves garlic, minced
- 1/4 cup chopped fresh parsley
- 1/4 cup chopped fresh mint
- 1/4 cup chopped green onions (scallions)
- 1/4 cup chopped cucumber
- 1/4 cup chopped tomatoes
- 1/4 cup chopped red bell pepper
- 1/4 cup chopped black olives
- 1/4 cup crumbled feta cheese (optional)
- Salt and black pepper, to taste
- Optional garnish: additional chopped fresh herbs, a drizzle of olive oil, and a sprinkle of paprika

Instructions:

Place the potato cubes in a large pot and cover them with cold water. Add a pinch of salt to the water. Bring the water to a boil over medium-high heat, then reduce the heat to medium-low and simmer for about 10-15 minutes, or until the potatoes are fork-tender but still hold their shape.

While the potatoes are cooking, prepare the dressing. In a small bowl, whisk together the Greek yogurt, tahini, lemon juice, minced garlic, chopped parsley, and chopped mint until smooth. Season with salt and black pepper to taste.

Once the potatoes are cooked, drain them in a colander and let them cool for a few minutes.

In a large mixing bowl, combine the cooked potatoes, chopped green onions, chopped cucumber, chopped tomatoes, chopped red bell pepper, and chopped black olives.

Pour the prepared dressing over the potato mixture in the bowl and toss gently to coat all the ingredients evenly.

If using, sprinkle crumbled feta cheese over the salad and toss lightly.

Taste the potato salad and adjust the seasoning if needed.

Transfer the Potato Salad with Middle Eastern Twist to a serving dish.

If desired, garnish with additional chopped fresh herbs, a drizzle of olive oil, and a sprinkle of paprika before serving.

Serve the potato salad immediately, or refrigerate for about 30 minutes to allow the flavors to meld together before serving.

Enjoy this delicious Potato Salad with a Middle Eastern twist as a side dish or a light meal!

Tuna Salad with Mediterranean Flavors

Ingredients:

- 2 cans (5 ounces each) of tuna in water, drained
- 1/4 cup chopped red onion
- 1/4 cup chopped cucumber
- 1/4 cup chopped cherry tomatoes
- 1/4 cup chopped Kalamata olives
- 2 tablespoons chopped fresh parsley
- 2 tablespoons chopped fresh basil
- 1 tablespoon capers, drained and chopped
- 2 tablespoons extra-virgin olive oil
- 1 tablespoon red wine vinegar
- 1 tablespoon lemon juice
- 1 teaspoon Dijon mustard
- Salt and black pepper, to taste
- Optional: crumbled feta cheese, chopped fresh mint, chopped roasted red peppers

Instructions:

In a large mixing bowl, combine the drained tuna, chopped red onion, chopped cucumber, chopped cherry tomatoes, chopped Kalamata olives, chopped parsley, chopped basil, and chopped capers.
In a small bowl, whisk together the extra-virgin olive oil, red wine vinegar, lemon juice, Dijon mustard, salt, and black pepper until well combined.
Pour the dressing over the tuna mixture in the large bowl and toss gently to coat all the ingredients evenly.
Taste the tuna salad and adjust the seasoning if needed.

If desired, add optional ingredients such as crumbled feta cheese, chopped fresh mint, or chopped roasted red peppers and toss gently to combine.

Transfer the Tuna Salad with Mediterranean Flavors to a serving dish.

Serve the tuna salad immediately, or refrigerate for about 30 minutes to allow the flavors to meld together before serving.

Enjoy this flavorful Tuna Salad with Mediterranean flavors as a light meal or a satisfying sandwich filling!

Spinach Salad with Pomegranate Dressing

Ingredients:

For the Salad:

- 6 cups baby spinach leaves, washed and dried
- 1/2 cup pomegranate seeds
- 1/4 cup crumbled feta cheese
- 1/4 cup sliced almonds, toasted
- 1/4 cup thinly sliced red onion

For the Pomegranate Dressing:

- 1/4 cup pomegranate juice
- 2 tablespoons balsamic vinegar
- 1 tablespoon honey
- 1 teaspoon Dijon mustard
- 1/4 cup extra-virgin olive oil
- Salt and black pepper, to taste

Instructions:

For the Salad:

In a large salad bowl, combine the baby spinach leaves, pomegranate seeds, crumbled feta cheese, sliced almonds, and thinly sliced red onion.

For the Pomegranate Dressing:

In a small bowl or a jar with a lid, whisk together the pomegranate juice, balsamic vinegar, honey, and Dijon mustard until well combined.

Slowly drizzle in the extra-virgin olive oil while whisking continuously to emulsify the dressing.

Season the dressing with salt and black pepper to taste, and adjust the sweetness or acidity if desired by adding more honey or vinegar.

Taste the dressing and adjust the seasoning to your preference.

Assembling the Salad:

Drizzle the desired amount of the pomegranate dressing over the salad in the bowl.

Toss the salad gently to coat all the ingredients evenly with the dressing.

Serve the Spinach Salad with Pomegranate Dressing immediately as a side dish or a light meal.

Enjoy this refreshing and flavorful salad with the unique twist of pomegranate dressing!

Radish Salad with Sumac Dressing

Ingredients:

For the Salad:

- 2 cups thinly sliced radishes
- 1/4 cup thinly sliced red onion
- 1/4 cup chopped fresh parsley
- 1/4 cup chopped fresh mint
- 1/4 cup crumbled feta cheese (optional)
- 2 tablespoons chopped walnuts (optional)

For the Sumac Dressing:

- 2 tablespoons extra-virgin olive oil
- 1 tablespoon lemon juice
- 1 teaspoon sumac powder
- 1 teaspoon honey
- Salt and black pepper, to taste

Instructions:

For the Salad:

In a large salad bowl, combine the thinly sliced radishes, thinly sliced red onion, chopped fresh parsley, and chopped fresh mint.
If using, add the crumbled feta cheese and chopped walnuts to the salad bowl.

For the Sumac Dressing:

> In a small bowl or a jar with a lid, whisk together the extra-virgin olive oil, lemon juice, sumac powder, and honey until well combined.
> Season the dressing with salt and black pepper to taste, and adjust the sweetness or acidity if desired by adding more honey or lemon juice.
> Taste the dressing and adjust the seasoning to your preference.

Assembling the Salad:

> Drizzle the desired amount of the sumac dressing over the salad in the bowl.
> Toss the salad gently to coat all the ingredients evenly with the dressing.
> Serve the Radish Salad with Sumac Dressing immediately as a side dish or a light meal.

Enjoy this refreshing and tangy salad with the unique flavor of sumac dressing!

Watermelon Salad with Feta Cheese

Ingredients:

- 4 cups cubed seedless watermelon
- 1/2 cup crumbled feta cheese
- 1/4 cup chopped fresh mint leaves
- 2 tablespoons extra-virgin olive oil
- 1 tablespoon balsamic vinegar (or to taste)
- Salt and black pepper, to taste

Instructions:

In a large serving bowl, combine the cubed watermelon, crumbled feta cheese, and chopped fresh mint leaves.
In a small bowl, whisk together the extra-virgin olive oil and balsamic vinegar to make the dressing. Adjust the ratio to your taste preference.
Drizzle the dressing over the watermelon, feta, and mint mixture.
Gently toss the salad until all ingredients are evenly coated with the dressing.
Season with salt and black pepper to taste.
Serve the Watermelon Salad with Feta Cheese immediately, or chill in the refrigerator for about 30 minutes before serving to allow the flavors to meld together.
Optionally, you can garnish with additional fresh mint leaves before serving.

Enjoy this refreshing and flavorful Watermelon Salad with Feta Cheese as a side dish or a light summer snack!

Orange and Olive Salad

Ingredients:

- 3-4 large oranges, peeled and sliced into rounds
- 1/2 cup pitted green olives, sliced
- 1/4 cup red onion, thinly sliced
- 2 tablespoons extra virgin olive oil
- 1 tablespoon lemon juice
- Salt and pepper to taste
- Fresh parsley or mint leaves for garnish (optional)

Instructions:

In a large bowl, combine the sliced oranges, sliced olives, and thinly sliced red onion.
In a small bowl, whisk together the extra virgin olive oil and lemon juice to make the dressing. Season with salt and pepper to taste.
Pour the dressing over the orange, olive, and onion mixture. Gently toss to coat everything evenly.
Let the salad marinate for about 10-15 minutes to allow the flavors to meld together.
Garnish with fresh parsley or mint leaves if desired before serving.

This salad offers a refreshing combination of sweet and tangy flavors from the oranges and olives, balanced with the brightness of lemon juice and the savory note from the olive oil. Enjoy!

Cauliflower Salad with Tahini Dressing

Ingredients:

For the Salad:

- 1 medium head of cauliflower, cut into small florets
- 1 tablespoon olive oil
- Salt and pepper, to taste
- 1/4 cup chopped fresh parsley
- 1/4 cup chopped fresh cilantro
- 1/4 cup chopped green onions
- 1/4 cup toasted pine nuts or sliced almonds (optional)
- 1/4 cup dried cranberries or raisins (optional)

For the Tahini Dressing:

- 1/4 cup tahini paste
- 2 tablespoons lemon juice
- 2 tablespoons water
- 1 garlic clove, minced
- 1/2 teaspoon ground cumin
- Salt and pepper, to taste

Instructions:

Preheat your oven to 400°F (200°C).

In a large bowl, toss the cauliflower florets with olive oil, salt, and pepper until evenly coated.

Spread the cauliflower florets in a single layer on a baking sheet lined with parchment paper. Roast in the preheated oven for 20-25 minutes or until the cauliflower is tender and lightly browned. Remove from the oven and let cool slightly.

While the cauliflower is roasting, prepare the tahini dressing. In a small bowl, whisk together tahini paste, lemon juice, water, minced garlic, ground cumin, salt, and pepper until smooth and creamy. Adjust the consistency with more water if needed.

Once the cauliflower has cooled slightly, transfer it to a large mixing bowl. Add chopped parsley, cilantro, green onions, toasted pine nuts or almonds, and dried cranberries or raisins (if using).

Drizzle the tahini dressing over the salad and gently toss until all the ingredients are well coated.

Taste and adjust the seasoning if necessary. You can add more lemon juice, salt, or pepper according to your preference.

Serve the cauliflower salad immediately, or chill it in the refrigerator for about 30 minutes to allow the flavors to meld together before serving.

This cauliflower salad with tahini dressing is packed with flavor and textures, making it a delicious and nutritious side dish or light meal. Enjoy!

Grilled Halloumi Salad

Ingredients:

For the Salad:

- 1 block of halloumi cheese, sliced into 1/4-inch thick slices
- 4 cups mixed salad greens (such as baby spinach, arugula, and/or lettuce)
- 1 cup cherry tomatoes, halved
- 1 cucumber, sliced
- 1 red bell pepper, sliced
- 1/4 cup sliced red onion
- 1/4 cup fresh herbs (such as parsley, mint, or basil), chopped
- Optional: olives, avocado slices, or any other desired salad ingredients

For the Dressing:

- 3 tablespoons extra virgin olive oil
- 1 tablespoon balsamic vinegar
- 1 tablespoon lemon juice
- 1 teaspoon Dijon mustard
- Salt and pepper to taste

Instructions:

Preheat a grill pan or outdoor grill over medium-high heat.
In a small bowl, whisk together the ingredients for the dressing: olive oil, balsamic vinegar, lemon juice, Dijon mustard, salt, and pepper. Set aside.

Grill the halloumi slices for 2-3 minutes on each side, or until grill marks appear and the cheese is softened. Remove from the grill and set aside.

In a large mixing bowl, combine the mixed salad greens, cherry tomatoes, cucumber slices, red bell pepper slices, sliced red onion, and chopped fresh herbs. Toss to combine.

Arrange the grilled halloumi slices on top of the salad.

Drizzle the dressing over the salad and halloumi slices.

Gently toss the salad to coat everything evenly with the dressing.

Taste and adjust the seasoning if necessary.

Serve the grilled halloumi salad immediately, garnished with additional fresh herbs if desired.

This Grilled Halloumi Salad is perfect as a light lunch or a flavorful side dish for grilled meats or seafood. Enjoy the combination of the salty halloumi cheese with the fresh, crisp vegetables and tangy dressing!

Avocado and Chickpea Salad

Ingredients:

- 1 can (15 ounces) chickpeas (garbanzo beans), drained and rinsed
- 2 ripe avocados, diced
- 1 cup cherry tomatoes, halved
- 1/4 cup red onion, finely chopped
- 1/4 cup fresh cilantro or parsley, chopped
- Juice of 1 lime
- 2 tablespoons extra virgin olive oil
- Salt and pepper to taste
- Optional: crumbled feta cheese, sliced cucumber, bell pepper, or any other desired salad ingredients

Instructions:

In a large mixing bowl, combine the drained and rinsed chickpeas, diced avocado, cherry tomatoes, chopped red onion, and chopped cilantro or parsley.
In a small bowl, whisk together the lime juice and extra virgin olive oil to make the dressing. Season with salt and pepper to taste.
Pour the dressing over the salad ingredients in the large mixing bowl.
Gently toss the salad until all the ingredients are evenly coated with the dressing.
Taste and adjust the seasoning if necessary.
If desired, add any optional salad ingredients such as crumbled feta cheese, sliced cucumber, or bell pepper.
Serve the avocado and chickpea salad immediately, or chill it in the refrigerator for about 30 minutes to allow the flavors to meld together before serving.

This Avocado and Chickpea Salad is perfect as a side dish or a light meal on its own.

Enjoy the creamy avocado, hearty chickpeas, and fresh flavors in every bite!

Quinoa Tabbouleh

Ingredients:

- 1 cup quinoa, rinsed
- 2 cups water or vegetable broth
- 1 cup cherry tomatoes, halved
- 1 cucumber, diced
- 1/2 cup red onion, finely chopped
- 1/2 cup fresh parsley, finely chopped
- 1/4 cup fresh mint leaves, finely chopped
- Juice of 2-3 lemons
- 1/4 cup extra virgin olive oil
- Salt and pepper to taste

Optional Additions:

- 1/4 cup chopped green onions
- 1/4 cup diced bell pepper (red, yellow, or green)
- 1/4 cup pitted Kalamata olives, chopped
- 1/4 cup crumbled feta cheese

Instructions:

In a medium saucepan, combine the rinsed quinoa and water or vegetable broth. Bring to a boil, then reduce the heat to low, cover, and simmer for 15-20 minutes, or until the quinoa is cooked and the liquid is absorbed. Remove from heat and let it cool.
In a large mixing bowl, combine the cooked quinoa, halved cherry tomatoes, diced cucumber, chopped red onion, chopped parsley, and chopped mint leaves.

In a small bowl, whisk together the lemon juice and extra virgin olive oil to make the dressing. Season with salt and pepper to taste.

Pour the dressing over the quinoa and vegetable mixture in the large mixing bowl. Gently toss the salad until all the ingredients are evenly coated with the dressing. Taste and adjust the seasoning if necessary.

If desired, add any optional additions such as chopped green onions, diced bell pepper, chopped Kalamata olives, or crumbled feta cheese.

Serve the quinoa tabbouleh immediately, or chill it in the refrigerator for about 30 minutes to allow the flavors to meld together before serving.

This Quinoa Tabbouleh is not only flavorful and refreshing but also packed with protein and nutrients. Enjoy it as a side dish, light meal, or a healthy addition to your lunch or dinner spread!

Labneh Salad with Mint and Olives

Ingredients:

- 1 cup labneh (strained yogurt cheese)
- 1/4 cup pitted olives (such as Kalamata or green olives), sliced
- 2 tablespoons fresh mint leaves, chopped
- 1 tablespoon extra virgin olive oil
- 1 tablespoon lemon juice
- Salt and pepper to taste
- Optional: sliced cucumber, cherry tomatoes, red onion, or any other desired salad ingredients

Instructions:

In a medium mixing bowl, combine the labneh, sliced olives, and chopped mint leaves.
In a small bowl, whisk together the extra virgin olive oil and lemon juice to make the dressing. Season with salt and pepper to taste.
Pour the dressing over the labneh mixture in the medium mixing bowl.
Gently toss the salad until all the ingredients are evenly coated with the dressing.
Taste and adjust the seasoning if necessary.
If desired, add any optional salad ingredients such as sliced cucumber, cherry tomatoes, or red onion.
Serve the Labneh Salad with Mint and Olives immediately, or chill it in the refrigerator for about 30 minutes to allow the flavors to meld together before serving.

This Labneh Salad with Mint and Olives is perfect as a side dish or a light appetizer. Enjoy the creamy texture of the labneh cheese combined with the fresh flavors of mint and olives!

Artichoke Salad

Ingredients:

- 2 cans (14 ounces each) artichoke hearts, drained and quartered
- 1/4 cup sun-dried tomatoes, chopped
- 1/4 cup Kalamata olives, sliced
- 1/4 cup red onion, thinly sliced
- 2 tablespoons fresh parsley, chopped
- 2 tablespoons extra virgin olive oil
- 1 tablespoon balsamic vinegar
- Salt and pepper to taste
- Optional: crumbled feta cheese, pine nuts, or chopped fresh basil

Instructions:

In a large mixing bowl, combine the quartered artichoke hearts, chopped sun-dried tomatoes, sliced Kalamata olives, thinly sliced red onion, and chopped fresh parsley.
In a small bowl, whisk together the extra virgin olive oil and balsamic vinegar to make the dressing. Season with salt and pepper to taste.
Pour the dressing over the artichoke mixture in the large mixing bowl.
Gently toss the salad until all the ingredients are evenly coated with the dressing. Taste and adjust the seasoning if necessary.
If desired, add any optional ingredients such as crumbled feta cheese, pine nuts, or chopped fresh basil.
Serve the Artichoke Salad immediately, or chill it in the refrigerator for about 30 minutes to allow the flavors to meld together before serving.

This Artichoke Salad is perfect as a side dish or a light meal on its own. Enjoy the combination of tender artichoke hearts, savory sun-dried tomatoes, briny Kalamata olives, and tangy dressing!

Green Bean Salad with Almonds

Ingredients:

- 1 pound green beans, trimmed
- 1/4 cup sliced almonds, toasted
- 2 tablespoons extra virgin olive oil
- 1 tablespoon red wine vinegar or balsamic vinegar
- 1 teaspoon Dijon mustard
- 1 clove garlic, minced
- Salt and pepper to taste
- Optional: chopped fresh parsley or basil for garnish

Instructions:

Bring a large pot of salted water to a boil. Add the trimmed green beans and cook for 3-4 minutes, or until the beans are crisp-tender. Drain the beans and immediately transfer them to a bowl of ice water to stop the cooking process. Once cooled, drain again and pat dry with paper towels.
In a small skillet, toast the sliced almonds over medium heat, stirring frequently, until they are lightly golden and fragrant. Remove from heat and set aside to cool.
In a small bowl, whisk together the extra virgin olive oil, red wine vinegar or balsamic vinegar, Dijon mustard, minced garlic, salt, and pepper to make the dressing.
In a large mixing bowl, toss the blanched green beans with the toasted sliced almonds.

Pour the dressing over the green beans and almonds in the mixing bowl. Toss until the beans and almonds are evenly coated with the dressing.
Taste and adjust the seasoning if necessary.
Transfer the Green Bean Salad to a serving platter or bowl.
If desired, garnish with chopped fresh parsley or basil before serving.

This Green Bean Salad with Almonds is perfect as a side dish or a light and healthy snack. Enjoy the combination of crisp-tender green beans, crunchy almonds, and tangy dressing!

Kale Salad with Za'atar Dressing

Ingredients:

For the Salad:

- 1 bunch kale, stems removed and leaves thinly sliced
- 1/4 cup cherry tomatoes, halved
- 1/4 cup cucumber, diced
- 1/4 cup red onion, thinly sliced
- 1/4 cup crumbled feta cheese (optional)
- 2 tablespoons toasted pine nuts or almonds (optional)
- 1 tablespoon chopped fresh mint (optional)

For the Za'atar Dressing:

- 3 tablespoons extra virgin olive oil
- 1 tablespoon lemon juice
- 1 teaspoon za'atar seasoning
- 1 teaspoon honey or maple syrup (optional)
- Salt and pepper to taste

Instructions:

In a large mixing bowl, combine the thinly sliced kale leaves, halved cherry tomatoes, diced cucumber, and thinly sliced red onion. If using, add crumbled feta cheese, toasted pine nuts or almonds, and chopped fresh mint.

In a small bowl, whisk together the extra virgin olive oil, lemon juice, za'atar seasoning, and honey or maple syrup (if using) to make the dressing. Season with salt and pepper to taste.

Pour the za'atar dressing over the kale salad mixture in the large mixing bowl. Gently massage the dressing into the kale leaves using your hands, ensuring that the leaves are evenly coated and slightly wilted.

Taste and adjust the seasoning if necessary.

Transfer the Kale Salad with Za'atar Dressing to a serving platter or bowl.

Serve immediately as a side dish or a light meal.

This Kale Salad with Za'atar Dressing is packed with flavor and nutrients, making it a delicious and healthy addition to any meal. Enjoy the combination of vibrant kale, zesty dressing, and aromatic za'atar seasoning!

Date and Walnut Salad

Ingredients:

- 1 cup pitted dates, chopped
- 1 cup walnuts, chopped
- 4 cups mixed salad greens (such as spinach, arugula, or mixed baby greens)
- 1/4 cup crumbled feta cheese (optional)
- 1/4 cup extra virgin olive oil
- 2 tablespoons balsamic vinegar
- Salt and pepper to taste

Instructions:

Prepare the Dressing:
- In a small bowl, whisk together the olive oil, balsamic vinegar, salt, and pepper until well combined. Set aside.

Prepare the Salad:
- In a large mixing bowl, combine the mixed salad greens, chopped dates, and chopped walnuts.
- If using, sprinkle the crumbled feta cheese over the salad.

Assemble the Salad:

- Drizzle the dressing over the salad mixture, tossing gently to coat all the ingredients evenly.

Serve:
- Transfer the salad to serving plates or a large salad bowl.
- Optionally, garnish with additional chopped walnuts or crumbled feta cheese on top.
- Serve immediately and enjoy!

Variations:

- Add Protein: To make it more filling, you can add grilled chicken strips, cooked shrimp, or sliced hard-boiled eggs.
- Extra Crunch: Toast the walnuts before adding them to the salad for an extra crunchy texture.
- Fresh Fruits: Incorporate fresh fruits like sliced apples, pears, or oranges to add more flavor and freshness to the salad.
- Leafy Greens: Experiment with different types of leafy greens based on your preference or what's available, such as kale or romaine lettuce.

Feel free to adjust the ingredients and quantities according to your taste preferences.

Enjoy your delicious date and walnut salad!

Bulgur Salad with Herbs

Ingredients:

- 1 cup bulgur wheat
- 2 cups water or vegetable broth
- 1 cup chopped fresh herbs (such as parsley, mint, and dill)
- 1 cucumber, diced
- 1 tomato, diced
- 1/2 red onion, finely chopped
- 1/4 cup lemon juice
- 1/4 cup extra virgin olive oil
- Salt and pepper to taste

Instructions:

Cook the Bulgur:
- In a saucepan, bring the water or vegetable broth to a boil.
- Stir in the bulgur wheat, cover, and remove from heat.
- Let it sit for about 15-20 minutes or until the bulgur is tender and has absorbed all the liquid.

- Fluff the bulgur with a fork and let it cool to room temperature.

Prepare the Dressing:
- In a small bowl, whisk together the lemon juice, extra virgin olive oil, salt, and pepper to make the dressing. Adjust seasoning to taste.

Assemble the Salad:
- In a large mixing bowl, combine the cooked bulgur, chopped fresh herbs, diced cucumber, diced tomato, and finely chopped red onion.

Toss with Dressing:
- Pour the dressing over the bulgur salad mixture.
- Gently toss until all the ingredients are evenly coated with the dressing.

Chill (Optional):
- You can chill the salad in the refrigerator for about 30 minutes to allow the flavors to meld together.

Serve:
- Transfer the bulgur salad to a serving dish or individual plates.
- Optionally, garnish with additional fresh herbs on top.
- Serve chilled or at room temperature as a side dish or light main course.

Variations:

- Add Protein: Boost the protein content by adding chickpeas, grilled chicken, or tofu cubes.
- Nuts and Seeds: For extra crunch and nutrition, sprinkle toasted pine nuts, almonds, or sunflower seeds over the salad.
- Feta Cheese: Crumble some feta cheese over the salad for a creamy and tangy addition.
- Roasted Vegetables: Toss in some roasted vegetables like bell peppers, zucchini, or eggplant for extra flavor and texture.

Feel free to customize the salad with your favorite herbs, vegetables, and additional toppings according to your taste preferences. Enjoy your flavorful bulgur salad with herbs!

Roasted Pepper Salad

Ingredients:

- 3 large bell peppers (red, yellow, and/or orange)
- 2 tablespoons extra virgin olive oil
- 2 cloves garlic, minced
- 1 tablespoon balsamic vinegar
- 1 teaspoon Dijon mustard
- Salt and pepper to taste
- 1/4 cup chopped fresh parsley or basil (optional, for garnish)
- Optional additional ingredients:
    - 1/4 cup sliced red onions
    - 1/4 cup crumbled feta cheese
    - 1/4 cup pitted olives (such as Kalamata or green olives)

Instructions:

Roast the Peppers:
- Preheat your oven to 425°F (220°C).

- Place the whole bell peppers on a baking sheet lined with parchment paper or aluminum foil.
- Roast the peppers in the preheated oven for about 25-30 minutes, or until the skins are blistered and charred, turning them occasionally to ensure even roasting.
- Remove the roasted peppers from the oven and transfer them to a heatproof bowl. Cover the bowl with plastic wrap or a kitchen towel and let the peppers steam for about 10 minutes. This will help loosen the skins.

Peel and Slice the Peppers:
- After steaming, carefully peel off the charred skins from the peppers. They should come off easily.
- Cut the peppers in half, remove the seeds and membranes, and slice them into thin strips.

Prepare the Dressing:
- In a small bowl, whisk together the extra virgin olive oil, minced garlic, balsamic vinegar, Dijon mustard, salt, and pepper to make the dressing. Adjust seasoning to taste.

Assemble the Salad:
- In a large mixing bowl, combine the roasted pepper strips with any additional ingredients you're using, such as sliced red onions, crumbled feta cheese, or pitted olives.

Toss with Dressing:
- Pour the dressing over the roasted pepper mixture in the bowl.
- Gently toss until all the ingredients are evenly coated with the dressing.

Serve:
- Transfer the roasted pepper salad to a serving dish.
- Optionally, garnish with chopped fresh parsley or basil on top.
- Serve the salad at room temperature or chilled as a delicious side dish or appetizer.

Variations:

- Herbs: Experiment with different herbs like thyme, oregano, or cilantro to add more flavor to the salad.
- Spices: Sprinkle some crushed red pepper flakes or smoked paprika for an extra kick of heat and flavor.
- Grains: Serve the roasted pepper salad over a bed of cooked quinoa, couscous, or bulgur wheat for a heartier meal.

- Nuts: Add some toasted pine nuts, almonds, or walnuts for additional texture and crunch.

Feel free to adjust the ingredients and quantities according to your taste preferences.

Enjoy your vibrant and flavorful roasted pepper salad!

Cabbage Salad with Lemon-Tahini Dressing

Ingredients:

For the Salad:

- 4 cups shredded green cabbage
- 1 cup shredded purple cabbage
- 1 large carrot, grated
- 1/4 cup chopped fresh parsley
- 1/4 cup sliced green onions (optional)
- 1/4 cup toasted sesame seeds (optional, for garnish)

For the Lemon-Tahini Dressing:

- 1/4 cup tahini (sesame seed paste)
- 1/4 cup fresh lemon juice
- 2 tablespoons extra virgin olive oil
- 2 cloves garlic, minced
- 1 tablespoon maple syrup or honey

- 2 tablespoons water, or more as needed
- Salt and pepper to taste

Instructions:

Prepare the Salad:
- In a large mixing bowl, combine the shredded green cabbage, shredded purple cabbage, grated carrot, chopped fresh parsley, and sliced green onions (if using). Toss until evenly mixed.

Prepare the Lemon-Tahini Dressing:
- In a small bowl, whisk together the tahini, fresh lemon juice, extra virgin olive oil, minced garlic, maple syrup or honey, and a pinch of salt and pepper until smooth.
- Gradually add water to the dressing, one tablespoon at a time, until you reach your desired consistency. The dressing should be creamy and pourable but not too thick.

Toss with Dressing:
- Pour the lemon-tahini dressing over the cabbage salad mixture in the large bowl.
- Gently toss until all the ingredients are evenly coated with the dressing.

Chill (Optional):
- You can chill the salad in the refrigerator for about 15-30 minutes to allow the flavors to meld together.

Serve:
- Transfer the cabbage salad to a serving dish or individual plates.
- Optionally, garnish with toasted sesame seeds on top.
- Serve the salad chilled or at room temperature as a refreshing side dish or light meal.

Variations:

- Add Protein: Boost the protein content by adding grilled chicken strips, cooked chickpeas, or tofu cubes to the salad.
- Crunchy Additions: Toss in some sliced almonds, chopped peanuts, or crispy fried wonton strips for extra crunch.
- Spice it Up: Add a pinch of red pepper flakes or a dash of Sriracha sauce to the dressing for a spicy kick.
- Fresh Herbs: Experiment with different herbs like cilantro, mint, or dill to add more flavor and freshness to the salad.

Feel free to customize the salad with your favorite ingredients and adjust the dressing according to your taste preferences. Enjoy your flavorful cabbage salad with lemon-tahini dressing!

Arugula Salad with Figs and Goat Cheese

Ingredients:

- 4 cups fresh arugula leaves
- 6 ripe figs, sliced
- 1/4 cup crumbled goat cheese
- 1/4 cup chopped toasted walnuts or pecans
- 2 tablespoons extra virgin olive oil
- 1 tablespoon balsamic vinegar
- 1 teaspoon honey or maple syrup
- Salt and freshly ground black pepper to taste

Instructions:

Prepare the Dressing:
- In a small bowl, whisk together the extra virgin olive oil, balsamic vinegar, honey or maple syrup, salt, and pepper until well combined. Set aside.

Assemble the Salad:
- In a large mixing bowl, combine the fresh arugula leaves, sliced figs, crumbled goat cheese, and chopped toasted walnuts or pecans.

Toss with Dressing:
- Pour the dressing over the salad mixture in the bowl.
- Gently toss until all the ingredients are evenly coated with the dressing.

Serve:
- Transfer the arugula salad to a serving dish or individual plates.
- Optionally, garnish with additional crumbled goat cheese and chopped toasted nuts on top.
- Serve the salad immediately as a refreshing appetizer or side dish.

Variations:

- Herbs: Add some chopped fresh mint or basil leaves for extra flavor and freshness.
- Protein: Make the salad more filling by adding grilled chicken strips, cooked shrimp, or sliced hard-boiled eggs.
- Dried Fruits: If fresh figs are not available, you can use dried figs rehydrated in warm water or other dried fruits like cranberries or apricots.
- Seeds: Sprinkle some toasted pumpkin seeds or sunflower seeds over the salad for additional texture and nutrition.

Feel free to adjust the ingredients and quantities according to your taste preferences.

Enjoy your delicious arugula salad with figs and goat cheese!

Zucchini Salad with Yogurt Dressing

Ingredients:

For the Salad:

- 2 medium zucchinis, thinly sliced
- 1/4 cup red onion, thinly sliced
- 1/4 cup cherry tomatoes, halved
- 1/4 cup crumbled feta cheese (optional)
- 2 tablespoons chopped fresh herbs (such as parsley, dill, or mint)
- Salt and pepper to taste

For the Yogurt Dressing:

- 1/2 cup Greek yogurt
- 1 tablespoon lemon juice
- 1 tablespoon extra virgin olive oil
- 1 clove garlic, minced

- 1 teaspoon honey or maple syrup (optional)
- Salt and pepper to taste

Instructions:

Prepare the Zucchini:
- Using a mandoline slicer or a sharp knife, thinly slice the zucchinis and red onion. Place them in a large mixing bowl.

Prepare the Dressing:
- In a small bowl, whisk together the Greek yogurt, lemon juice, extra virgin olive oil, minced garlic, honey or maple syrup (if using), salt, and pepper until smooth and well combined.

Assemble the Salad:
- Pour the yogurt dressing over the sliced zucchinis and red onion in the mixing bowl.
- Add the cherry tomatoes, crumbled feta cheese (if using), and chopped fresh herbs.
- Toss gently until all the ingredients are evenly coated with the dressing.

Chill (Optional):
- You can chill the salad in the refrigerator for about 15-30 minutes to allow the flavors to meld together.

Serve:
- Transfer the zucchini salad to a serving dish or individual plates.
- Optionally, garnish with additional chopped herbs on top.
- Serve the salad chilled or at room temperature as a delicious side dish or light meal.

Variations:

- Grilled Zucchini: For added flavor, you can grill the zucchini slices before assembling the salad.
- Nuts or Seeds: Sprinkle some toasted pine nuts, almonds, or sunflower seeds over the salad for extra crunch.
- Spices: Add a pinch of paprika, cumin, or chili powder to the dressing for a hint of spice.
- Fresh Vegetables: Feel free to add other fresh vegetables like cucumber, bell peppers, or radishes to the salad for more variety.

Feel free to customize the salad with your favorite ingredients and adjust the dressing according to your taste preferences. Enjoy your delicious zucchini salad with yogurt dressing!

Pistachio and Cranberry Couscous Salad

Ingredients:

- 1 cup couscous
- 1 1/4 cups vegetable broth or water
- 1/2 cup shelled pistachios, chopped
- 1/2 cup dried cranberries
- 1/4 cup chopped fresh parsley
- 2 tablespoons extra virgin olive oil
- 2 tablespoons lemon juice
- 1 teaspoon honey or maple syrup
- Salt and pepper to taste

Instructions:

Prepare the Couscous:

- In a saucepan, bring the vegetable broth or water to a boil.
- Stir in the couscous, cover the saucepan, and remove it from the heat.
- Let the couscous sit for about 5 minutes, or until it has absorbed all the liquid.
- Fluff the couscous with a fork to separate the grains and let it cool to room temperature.

Prepare the Dressing:
- In a small bowl, whisk together the extra virgin olive oil, lemon juice, honey or maple syrup, salt, and pepper to make the dressing. Adjust seasoning to taste.

Assemble the Salad:
- In a large mixing bowl, combine the cooked and cooled couscous, chopped pistachios, dried cranberries, and chopped fresh parsley.

Toss with Dressing:
- Pour the dressing over the couscous salad mixture in the bowl.
- Gently toss until all the ingredients are evenly coated with the dressing.

Chill (Optional):
- You can chill the salad in the refrigerator for about 30 minutes to allow the flavors to meld together.

Serve:
- Transfer the pistachio and cranberry couscous salad to a serving dish or individual plates.
- Optionally, garnish with additional chopped parsley or whole pistachios on top.
- Serve the salad chilled or at room temperature as a flavorful side dish or light meal.

Variations:

- Herbs: Experiment with different herbs like mint or cilantro for added freshness and flavor.
- Cheese: Add crumbled feta cheese or goat cheese for a creamy tanginess.
- Vegetables: Mix in some diced cucumber, cherry tomatoes, or bell peppers for extra color and crunch.
- Citrus: Substitute orange juice for the lemon juice in the dressing for a citrusy twist.

Feel free to adjust the ingredients and quantities according to your taste preferences.

Enjoy your delicious pistachio and cranberry couscous salad!

Tzatziki Cucumber Salad

Ingredients:

- 2 large cucumbers, thinly sliced
- 1/2 cup Greek yogurt
- 1/4 cup sour cream or Greek yogurt (for extra creaminess)
- 2 cloves garlic, minced
- 1 tablespoon extra virgin olive oil
- 1 tablespoon fresh lemon juice
- 1 tablespoon chopped fresh dill (or mint)
- 1 tablespoon chopped fresh parsley
- Salt and pepper to taste
- Optional: 1/4 cup crumbled feta cheese, for garnish

Instructions:

Prepare the Cucumbers:

- Slice the cucumbers thinly using a mandoline slicer or a sharp knife. You can also use a vegetable peeler to create ribbons.

Make the Tzatziki Dressing:
- In a mixing bowl, combine the Greek yogurt, sour cream or additional Greek yogurt, minced garlic, extra virgin olive oil, lemon juice, chopped fresh dill (or mint), and chopped fresh parsley. Mix until well combined.
- Season the dressing with salt and pepper to taste. Adjust seasoning as needed.

Assemble the Salad:
- Add the thinly sliced cucumbers to the bowl with the tzatziki dressing.
- Gently toss the cucumbers with the dressing until they are well coated.

Chill (Optional):
- You can chill the cucumber salad in the refrigerator for about 15-30 minutes to allow the flavors to meld together and the cucumbers to marinate slightly.

Serve:
- Transfer the tzatziki cucumber salad to a serving dish or individual plates.
- Optionally, garnish with crumbled feta cheese on top for extra flavor and creaminess.
- Serve the salad chilled as a refreshing side dish or appetizer.

Variations:

- Herbs: Feel free to customize the salad with your favorite herbs. Besides dill and parsley, you can use cilantro, basil, or oregano.
- Additions: Mix in chopped tomatoes, red onions, olives, or bell peppers for additional flavor and texture.
- Spices: Add a pinch of paprika, cumin, or dried oregano to the dressing for a hint of Mediterranean spice.
- Vegan Option: Use dairy-free yogurt or sour cream alternatives to make the salad vegan-friendly.

Feel free to adjust the ingredients and quantities according to your taste preferences. Enjoy your delicious tzatziki cucumber salad!

Carrot and Raisin Salad

Ingredients:

- 4 cups grated carrots (about 4-6 medium carrots)
- 1/2 cup raisins
- 1/4 cup chopped walnuts or pecans (optional, for extra crunch)
- 1/4 cup mayonnaise
- 2 tablespoons Greek yogurt or sour cream (for extra creaminess)
- 1 tablespoon honey or maple syrup
- 1 tablespoon lemon juice
- 1 teaspoon Dijon mustard
- Salt and pepper to taste
- Optional: 1 tablespoon chopped fresh parsley or cilantro, for garnish

Instructions:

    Prepare the Carrots:

- Wash and peel the carrots, then grate them using a box grater or a food processor fitted with a grating attachment. Place the grated carrots in a large mixing bowl.

Add Raisins and Nuts:
- Add the raisins and chopped walnuts or pecans (if using) to the bowl with the grated carrots. Toss to combine.

Make the Dressing:
- In a small bowl, whisk together the mayonnaise, Greek yogurt or sour cream, honey or maple syrup, lemon juice, Dijon mustard, salt, and pepper until smooth and well combined.

Combine Dressing with Carrot Mixture:
- Pour the dressing over the carrot, raisin, and nut mixture in the large bowl.
- Gently toss until all the ingredients are evenly coated with the dressing.

Chill (Optional):
- You can chill the carrot and raisin salad in the refrigerator for about 15-30 minutes to allow the flavors to meld together.

Serve:
- Transfer the salad to a serving dish or individual plates.
- Optionally, garnish with chopped fresh parsley or cilantro on top.
- Serve the salad chilled as a delicious side dish or light snack.

Variations:

- Apples or Pineapple: Add diced apples or pineapple chunks for extra sweetness and flavor.
- Coconut: Mix in shredded coconut for a tropical twist.
- Spices: Add a pinch of cinnamon or nutmeg for warm, cozy flavors.
- Seeds: Sprinkle toasted sesame seeds or sunflower seeds over the salad for extra crunch.

Feel free to adjust the ingredients and quantities according to your taste preferences. Enjoy your delicious carrot and raisin salad!

Chickpea and Spinach Salad

Ingredients:

- 1 can (15 ounces) chickpeas, drained and rinsed
- 4 cups fresh spinach leaves, washed and chopped
- 1/2 red onion, thinly sliced
- 1/2 cup cherry tomatoes, halved
- 1/4 cup crumbled feta cheese (optional)
- 1/4 cup chopped fresh parsley or basil
- 2 tablespoons extra virgin olive oil
- 1 tablespoon balsamic vinegar
- 1 teaspoon Dijon mustard
- 1 clove garlic, minced
- Salt and pepper to taste

Instructions:

    Prepare the Dressing:

- In a small bowl, whisk together the extra virgin olive oil, balsamic vinegar, Dijon mustard, minced garlic, salt, and pepper until well combined. Set aside.

Assemble the Salad:
- In a large mixing bowl, combine the drained and rinsed chickpeas, chopped fresh spinach leaves, thinly sliced red onion, halved cherry tomatoes, and crumbled feta cheese (if using).
- Add the chopped fresh parsley or basil to the bowl.

Toss with Dressing:
- Pour the dressing over the chickpea and spinach mixture in the bowl.
- Gently toss until all the ingredients are evenly coated with the dressing.

Chill (Optional):
- You can chill the salad in the refrigerator for about 15-30 minutes to allow the flavors to meld together.

Serve:
- Transfer the chickpea and spinach salad to a serving dish or individual plates.
- Optionally, garnish with additional crumbled feta cheese or chopped fresh herbs on top.
- Serve the salad chilled or at room temperature as a delicious side dish or light meal.

Variations:

- Grains: Add cooked quinoa, bulgur wheat, or couscous to make the salad more filling.
- Nuts or Seeds: Sprinkle toasted almonds, pine nuts, or sunflower seeds over the salad for extra crunch.
- Avocado: Add sliced avocado for creaminess and extra nutrients.
- Dried Fruits: Mix in dried cranberries, raisins, or chopped apricots for a touch of sweetness.

Feel free to adjust the ingredients and quantities according to your taste preferences. Enjoy your flavorful chickpea and spinach salad!

Watercress Salad with Citrus Dressing

Ingredients:

For the Salad:

- 4 cups watercress, tough stems removed
- 1 orange, segmented
- 1 grapefruit, segmented
- 1/4 cup thinly sliced red onion
- 1/4 cup sliced almonds, toasted
- Optional: 1/4 cup crumbled feta cheese or goat cheese

For the Citrus Dressing:

- 1/4 cup fresh orange juice
- 2 tablespoons fresh grapefruit juice
- 2 tablespoons extra virgin olive oil
- 1 tablespoon honey or maple syrup

- 1 teaspoon Dijon mustard
- Salt and pepper to taste

Instructions:

Prepare the Citrus Dressing:
- In a small bowl, whisk together the fresh orange juice, fresh grapefruit juice, extra virgin olive oil, honey or maple syrup, Dijon mustard, salt, and pepper until well combined. Set aside.

Assemble the Salad:
- In a large mixing bowl, combine the watercress, segmented orange, segmented grapefruit, thinly sliced red onion, and sliced almonds.
- If using, add the crumbled feta cheese or goat cheese to the bowl.

Toss with Dressing:
- Pour the citrus dressing over the watercress salad mixture in the bowl.
- Gently toss until all the ingredients are evenly coated with the dressing.

Serve:
- Transfer the watercress salad to a serving dish or individual plates.
- Optionally, garnish with additional sliced almonds or crumbled cheese on top.
- Serve the salad immediately as a refreshing side dish or light meal.

Variations:

- Protein: Add grilled chicken, shrimp, or tofu cubes for added protein.
- Avocado: Include sliced avocado for creaminess and extra nutrients.
- Fresh Herbs: Toss in chopped fresh mint or basil leaves for additional flavor and freshness.
- Citrus Zest: Sprinkle some grated orange or grapefruit zest over the salad for extra citrusy aroma.

Feel free to adjust the ingredients and quantities according to your taste preferences. Enjoy your flavorful watercress salad with citrus dressing!

Millet Salad with Roasted Vegetables

Ingredients:

For the Roasted Vegetables:

- 2 cups diced vegetables (such as bell peppers, zucchini, eggplant, cherry tomatoes, carrots, and red onion)
- 2 tablespoons olive oil
- Salt and pepper to taste
- Optional: garlic powder, dried herbs (such as thyme or rosemary)

For the Millet:

- 1 cup millet
- 2 cups vegetable broth or water
- Salt to taste

For the Dressing:

- 3 tablespoons extra virgin olive oil
- 2 tablespoons balsamic vinegar
- 1 tablespoon maple syrup or honey
- 1 teaspoon Dijon mustard
- Salt and pepper to taste

Additional Ingredients:

- 1/4 cup chopped fresh parsley or basil
- 1/4 cup toasted pine nuts or almonds
- Optional: crumbled feta cheese or goat cheese

Instructions:

Roast the Vegetables:
- Preheat the oven to 400°F (200°C).
- In a large bowl, toss the diced vegetables with olive oil, salt, pepper, and any optional seasonings or herbs.
- Spread the vegetables in a single layer on a baking sheet lined with parchment paper.
- Roast in the preheated oven for 20-25 minutes, or until the vegetables are tender and slightly caramelized. Remove from the oven and let cool.

Cook the Millet:
- Rinse the millet under cold water using a fine mesh strainer.
- In a saucepan, bring the vegetable broth or water to a boil. Stir in the rinsed millet and a pinch of salt.
- Reduce the heat to low, cover, and simmer for about 15-20 minutes, or until the millet is tender and has absorbed all the liquid.
- Remove from heat and let the millet rest, covered, for 5 minutes. Fluff with a fork and let cool slightly.

Prepare the Dressing:
- In a small bowl, whisk together the extra virgin olive oil, balsamic vinegar, maple syrup or honey, Dijon mustard, salt, and pepper until well combined. Set aside.

Assemble the Salad:
- In a large mixing bowl, combine the cooked millet, roasted vegetables, chopped fresh parsley or basil, and toasted pine nuts or almonds.

- Pour the dressing over the salad mixture and toss until all the ingredients are evenly coated.

Serve:
- Transfer the millet salad to a serving dish or individual plates.
- Optionally, sprinkle crumbled feta cheese or goat cheese on top.
- Serve the salad warm or at room temperature as a satisfying main dish or side dish.

Variations:

- Herbs: Experiment with different herbs like cilantro, mint, or dill for added flavor.
- Protein: Add cooked chickpeas, grilled chicken, or tofu cubes to make the salad more filling.
- Dried Fruits: Mix in chopped dried apricots, cranberries, or raisins for a hint of sweetness.
- Greens: Serve the salad over a bed of mixed greens or spinach for extra freshness.

Feel free to customize the salad with your favorite vegetables and toppings. Enjoy your delicious millet salad with roasted vegetables!

Egg Salad with Middle Eastern Spices

Ingredients:

- 6 hard-boiled eggs, peeled and chopped
- 1/4 cup mayonnaise
- 1 tablespoon Greek yogurt or sour cream
- 1 teaspoon ground cumin
- 1/2 teaspoon ground coriander
- 1/2 teaspoon smoked paprika
- 1/4 teaspoon ground turmeric
- 1/4 teaspoon ground cinnamon
- Salt and pepper to taste
- 2 tablespoons chopped fresh cilantro or parsley
- Optional: chopped green onions or diced red onion for added flavor and crunch

Instructions:

Prepare the Hard-Boiled Eggs:
- Place the eggs in a saucepan and cover them with water.
- Bring the water to a boil over medium-high heat, then reduce the heat to low and simmer for 10-12 minutes.
- Remove the eggs from the hot water and transfer them to a bowl of ice water to cool completely. Once cooled, peel the eggs and chop them into bite-sized pieces.

Make the Middle Eastern Spice Blend:
- In a small bowl, combine the ground cumin, ground coriander, smoked paprika, ground turmeric, and ground cinnamon. Mix well to create the Middle Eastern spice blend.

Prepare the Dressing:
- In a large mixing bowl, whisk together the mayonnaise, Greek yogurt or sour cream, and 1 tablespoon of the Middle Eastern spice blend until smooth and well combined. Adjust seasoning with salt and pepper to taste.

Combine the Ingredients:
- Add the chopped hard-boiled eggs to the bowl with the dressing.
- Add the chopped fresh cilantro or parsley to the bowl.
- If using, add chopped green onions or diced red onion to the bowl for additional flavor and crunch.

Mix Well:
- Gently fold the ingredients together until the eggs are evenly coated with the dressing and spices.

Chill (Optional):
- You can chill the egg salad in the refrigerator for about 30 minutes to allow the flavors to meld together.

Serve:
- Transfer the egg salad to a serving dish.
- Optionally, garnish with additional chopped cilantro or parsley on top.
- Serve the Middle Eastern-spiced egg salad on its own, or as a sandwich filling, wrap filling, or on top of greens as a salad.

Variations:

- Add Heat: For a spicy kick, add a pinch of cayenne pepper or a dash of hot sauce to the dressing.

- Nuts and Seeds: Mix in toasted pine nuts, almonds, or sesame seeds for extra texture and flavor.
- Pickles: Fold in chopped pickles or pickled jalapeños for tanginess and crunch.
- Yogurt Options: Experiment with different types of yogurt, such as Greek yogurt, plain yogurt, or labneh, for variation in flavor and creaminess.

Feel free to adjust the ingredients and quantities according to your taste preferences. Enjoy your Middle Eastern-spiced egg salad!

Radicchio and Orange Salad

Ingredients:

- 1 head of radicchio, thinly sliced
- 2 oranges, peeled and segmented
- 1/4 cup pomegranate arils (optional, for extra color and sweetness)
- 1/4 cup chopped toasted walnuts or pecans
- 2 tablespoons extra virgin olive oil
- 1 tablespoon balsamic vinegar
- 1 teaspoon honey or maple syrup
- Salt and pepper to taste
- Optional: crumbled feta cheese or goat cheese for garnish
- Optional: chopped fresh parsley or mint for garnish

Instructions:

- Prepare the Radicchio:
  - Wash the radicchio and remove any wilted outer leaves. Cut the head of radicchio in half, then thinly slice it crosswise into strips. Place the sliced radicchio in a large mixing bowl.
- Prepare the Oranges:
  - Peel the oranges and remove any white pith. Slice between the membranes to segment the oranges, collecting the segments in a bowl.
- Assemble the Salad:
  - Add the orange segments to the bowl with the sliced radicchio.
  - If using, add the pomegranate arils to the bowl.
  - Sprinkle the chopped toasted walnuts or pecans over the salad ingredients.
- Make the Dressing:
  - In a small bowl, whisk together the extra virgin olive oil, balsamic vinegar, honey or maple syrup, salt, and pepper until well combined.
- Toss with Dressing:
  - Drizzle the dressing over the radicchio and orange salad mixture in the bowl.
  - Gently toss until all the ingredients are evenly coated with the dressing.
- Serve:
  - Transfer the salad to a serving dish or individual plates.
  - Optionally, garnish with crumbled feta cheese or goat cheese and chopped fresh parsley or mint on top.
  - Serve the salad immediately as a refreshing side dish or appetizer.

Variations:

- Greens: Add mixed greens like arugula or spinach to the salad for extra texture and flavor.
- Citrus: Experiment with different types of citrus fruits like grapefruit, blood oranges, or tangerines.
- Nuts: Substitute the toasted walnuts or pecans with toasted almonds, pine nuts, or pistachios.
- Dried Fruits: Include dried cranberries, apricots, or figs for additional sweetness and chewiness.

Feel free to adjust the ingredients and quantities according to your taste preferences. Enjoy your vibrant and flavorful radicchio and orange salad!

Black Bean Salad with Cilantro-Lime Dressing

Ingredients:

For the Salad:

- 2 cans (15 ounces each) black beans, drained and rinsed
- 1 red bell pepper, diced
- 1 yellow bell pepper, diced
- 1 cup cherry tomatoes, halved
- 1/2 cup red onion, finely chopped
- 1/4 cup fresh cilantro, chopped
- Optional: 1 jalapeño pepper, seeded and diced (for added heat)
- Optional: 1 avocado, diced

For the Cilantro-Lime Dressing:

- 1/4 cup fresh lime juice (about 2-3 limes)
- 2 tablespoons extra virgin olive oil
- 2 tablespoons chopped fresh cilantro
- 1 clove garlic, minced
- 1 teaspoon honey or maple syrup
- 1/2 teaspoon ground cumin
- Salt and pepper to taste

Instructions:

Prepare the Dressing:
- In a small bowl, whisk together the fresh lime juice, extra virgin olive oil, chopped fresh cilantro, minced garlic, honey or maple syrup, ground cumin, salt, and pepper until well combined. Set aside.

Assemble the Salad:
- In a large mixing bowl, combine the drained and rinsed black beans, diced red bell pepper, diced yellow bell pepper, halved cherry tomatoes, finely chopped red onion, and chopped fresh cilantro.
- If using, add the diced jalapeño pepper for added heat.

Toss with Dressing:
- Pour the cilantro-lime dressing over the black bean salad mixture in the bowl.
- Gently toss until all the ingredients are evenly coated with the dressing.

Chill (Optional):
- You can chill the salad in the refrigerator for about 15-30 minutes to allow the flavors to meld together.

Serve:
- Transfer the black bean salad to a serving dish or individual plates.
- If using, add the diced avocado to the salad.
- Serve the salad chilled or at room temperature as a refreshing side dish or light meal.

Variations:

- Grains: Add cooked quinoa, brown rice, or couscous to the salad for added texture and fiber.
- Protein: Mix in grilled chicken, shrimp, or tofu cubes for extra protein.
- Corn: Include fresh or grilled corn kernels for sweetness and crunch.

- Cheese: Sprinkle crumbled feta cheese or cotija cheese over the salad for additional flavor.

Feel free to adjust the ingredients and quantities according to your taste preferences. Enjoy your delicious black bean salad with cilantro-lime dressing!

Mushroom Salad with Balsamic Glaze

Ingredients:

- 1 pound mixed mushrooms (such as button mushrooms, cremini mushrooms, or shiitake mushrooms), cleaned and sliced
- 2 tablespoons olive oil
- 2 cloves garlic, minced
- Salt and pepper to taste
- 4 cups mixed salad greens (such as arugula, spinach, or mixed baby greens)
- 1/4 cup cherry tomatoes, halved
- 1/4 cup thinly sliced red onion
- Optional: 1/4 cup crumbled feta cheese or goat cheese

For the Balsamic Glaze:

- 1/2 cup balsamic vinegar
- 1 tablespoon honey or maple syrup

Instructions:

Prepare the Balsamic Glaze:
- In a small saucepan, combine the balsamic vinegar and honey or maple syrup.
- Bring the mixture to a simmer over medium heat, then reduce the heat to low.
- Simmer for about 10-15 minutes, stirring occasionally, until the glaze has thickened and reduced by half. Remove from heat and let cool.

Saute the Mushrooms:
- Heat olive oil in a large skillet over medium heat. Add the minced garlic and sauté for about 1 minute until fragrant.
- Add the sliced mushrooms to the skillet, season with salt and pepper, and sauté for 8-10 minutes, or until the mushrooms are tender and golden brown. Remove from heat and let cool slightly.

Assemble the Salad:
- In a large mixing bowl, combine the mixed salad greens, halved cherry tomatoes, thinly sliced red onion, and sautéed mushrooms.
- If using, sprinkle crumbled feta cheese or goat cheese over the salad ingredients.

Drizzle with Balsamic Glaze:
- Drizzle the cooled balsamic glaze over the salad.
- Toss gently to coat all the ingredients with the glaze.

Serve:
- Transfer the mushroom salad with balsamic glaze to a serving dish or individual plates.
- Optionally, garnish with additional freshly ground black pepper and a drizzle of extra balsamic glaze on top.
- Serve the salad immediately as a delicious appetizer or side dish.

Variations:

- Nuts: Add toasted pine nuts, walnuts, or almonds for extra crunch.
- Herbs: Toss in chopped fresh parsley, basil, or thyme for added freshness and flavor.
- Protein: Top the salad with grilled chicken strips, shrimp, or tofu cubes for added protein.

- Greens: Experiment with different salad greens like butter lettuce, kale, or frisée.

Feel free to customize the salad with your favorite ingredients and adjust the balsamic glaze according to your taste preferences. Enjoy your flavorful mushroom salad with balsamic glaze!

Roasted Tomato Salad

Ingredients:

- 1 pound cherry or grape tomatoes, halved
- 2 tablespoons olive oil
- 2 cloves garlic, minced
- 1 teaspoon dried oregano
- Salt and pepper to taste
- 4 cups mixed salad greens (such as arugula, spinach, or mixed baby greens)
- 1/4 cup thinly sliced red onion
- 1/4 cup crumbled feta cheese or goat cheese (optional)
- Balsamic glaze or vinegar, for drizzling (optional)
- Fresh basil leaves, for garnish (optional)

Instructions:

Preheat the Oven:
- Preheat your oven to 400°F (200°C).

Roast the Tomatoes:
- In a large mixing bowl, toss the halved cherry or grape tomatoes with olive oil, minced garlic, dried oregano, salt, and pepper until well coated.
- Spread the seasoned tomatoes in a single layer on a baking sheet lined with parchment paper.
- Roast in the preheated oven for 20-25 minutes, or until the tomatoes are softened and slightly caramelized. Remove from the oven and let cool slightly.

Assemble the Salad:
- In a large serving bowl, combine the mixed salad greens and thinly sliced red onion.
- Add the roasted tomatoes to the bowl, along with any juices from the baking sheet.

Add Cheese (Optional):
- If using, sprinkle crumbled feta cheese or goat cheese over the salad.

Drizzle with Balsamic Glaze (Optional):
- Drizzle balsamic glaze or vinegar over the salad for extra flavor and sweetness.

Garnish and Serve:
- Garnish the salad with fresh basil leaves for a burst of freshness and aroma.
- Serve the roasted tomato salad immediately as a delicious appetizer or side dish.

Variations:

- Herbs: Add chopped fresh basil, parsley, or thyme to the salad for extra flavor.
- Nuts: Sprinkle toasted pine nuts, walnuts, or almonds over the salad for added crunch.
- Protein: Top the salad with grilled chicken strips, shrimp, or tofu cubes for a more filling meal.
- Greens: Experiment with different salad greens like romaine lettuce, kale, or watercress.

Feel free to customize the salad with your favorite ingredients and adjust the seasoning according to your taste preferences. Enjoy your flavorful roasted tomato salad!

Asparagus Salad with Lemon-Parmesan Dressing

Ingredients:

For the Salad:

- 1 pound asparagus spears, tough ends trimmed
- 2 tablespoons olive oil
- Salt and pepper to taste
- 4 cups mixed salad greens (such as arugula, spinach, or mixed baby greens)
- 1/4 cup cherry tomatoes, halved
- 1/4 cup thinly sliced red onion
- Optional: 1/4 cup toasted pine nuts or sliced almonds

For the Lemon-Parmesan Dressing:

- 1/4 cup extra virgin olive oil
- 2 tablespoons freshly squeezed lemon juice
- 1 tablespoon grated Parmesan cheese
- 1 clove garlic, minced
- 1 teaspoon Dijon mustard
- Salt and pepper to taste

Instructions:

Prepare the Asparagus:
- Preheat your grill or grill pan over medium-high heat.
- Drizzle the trimmed asparagus spears with olive oil and season with salt and pepper.
- Grill the asparagus for 3-4 minutes per side, or until tender and slightly charred. Remove from the grill and let cool slightly.

Make the Dressing:
- In a small bowl, whisk together the extra virgin olive oil, freshly squeezed lemon juice, grated Parmesan cheese, minced garlic, Dijon mustard, salt, and pepper until well combined.

Assemble the Salad:
- In a large serving bowl, combine the mixed salad greens, halved cherry tomatoes, and thinly sliced red onion.
- Arrange the grilled asparagus spears on top of the salad greens.

Drizzle with Dressing:
- Drizzle the lemon-Parmesan dressing over the salad and grilled asparagus.

Add Nuts (Optional):
- If using, sprinkle toasted pine nuts or sliced almonds over the salad for added crunch and flavor.

Serve:
- Serve the asparagus salad with lemon-Parmesan dressing immediately as a delicious appetizer or side dish.

Variations:

- Herbs: Add chopped fresh basil, parsley, or thyme to the dressing for extra freshness and flavor.
- Cheese: Substitute grated Pecorino Romano or Asiago cheese for the Parmesan cheese in the dressing.

- Protein: Top the salad with grilled chicken strips, shrimp, or sliced hard-boiled eggs for added protein.
- Greens: Experiment with different salad greens like butter lettuce, kale, or watercress.

Feel free to customize the salad with your favorite ingredients and adjust the dressing according to your taste preferences. Enjoy your flavorful asparagus salad with lemon-Parmesan dressing!

Lentil and Roasted Vegetable Salad

Ingredients:

For the Roasted Vegetables:

- 2 cups chopped vegetables (such as bell peppers, zucchini, eggplant, cherry tomatoes, carrots, and red onion)
- 2 tablespoons olive oil
- 2 cloves garlic, minced
- Salt and pepper to taste
- Optional: dried herbs (such as thyme or rosemary)

For the Lentils:

- 1 cup dry lentils (green or brown), rinsed and drained

- 3 cups vegetable broth or water
- 1 bay leaf
- Salt to taste

For the Dressing:

- 1/4 cup extra virgin olive oil
- 2 tablespoons balsamic vinegar
- 1 tablespoon Dijon mustard
- 1 clove garlic, minced
- Salt and pepper to taste

Additional Ingredients:

- 4 cups mixed salad greens (such as arugula, spinach, or mixed baby greens)
- 1/4 cup crumbled feta cheese or goat cheese (optional)
- 2 tablespoons chopped fresh parsley or basil for garnish

Instructions:

Roast the Vegetables:
- Preheat your oven to 400°F (200°C).
- In a large mixing bowl, toss the chopped vegetables with olive oil, minced garlic, salt, pepper, and any optional dried herbs until well coated.
- Spread the seasoned vegetables in a single layer on a baking sheet lined with parchment paper.
- Roast in the preheated oven for 20-25 minutes, or until the vegetables are tender and slightly caramelized. Remove from the oven and let cool slightly.

Cook the Lentils:
- In a saucepan, combine the rinsed lentils, vegetable broth or water, and bay leaf.
- Bring the mixture to a boil, then reduce the heat to low and simmer, covered, for 20-25 minutes, or until the lentils are tender but still hold their shape.
- Remove from heat, discard the bay leaf, and season the lentils with salt to taste. Let cool slightly.

Prepare the Dressing:
- In a small bowl, whisk together the extra virgin olive oil, balsamic vinegar, Dijon mustard, minced garlic, salt, and pepper until well combined. Set aside.

Assemble the Salad:
- In a large serving bowl, combine the cooked lentils and roasted vegetables.
- Add the mixed salad greens to the bowl and gently toss to combine.

Drizzle with Dressing:
- Drizzle the prepared dressing over the lentil and roasted vegetable salad.

Add Cheese (Optional):
- If using, sprinkle crumbled feta cheese or goat cheese over the salad.

Garnish and Serve:
- Garnish the salad with chopped fresh parsley or basil for a burst of freshness.
- Serve the lentil and roasted vegetable salad immediately as a satisfying main dish or side dish.

Variations:

- Grains: Add cooked quinoa, bulgur wheat, or farro to the salad for extra texture and protein.
- Nuts: Sprinkle toasted pine nuts, almonds, or walnuts over the salad for added crunch.
- Herbs: Toss in chopped fresh dill, cilantro, or mint for additional flavor.
- Dried Fruits: Mix in chopped dried apricots, cranberries, or raisins for a hint of sweetness.

Feel free to customize the salad with your favorite ingredients and adjust the dressing according to your taste preferences. Enjoy your flavorful lentil and roasted vegetable salad!